Ripley Readers

Learning to read. Reading to learn!

LEVEL ONE Sounding It Out Preschool-Kindergarten
For kids who know their alphabet and are starting to sound out words.

learning sight words • beginning reading • sounding out words

LEVEL TWO Reading with Help Preschool-Grade 1
For kids who know sight words and are learning to sound out new words.

expanding vocabulary • building confidence • sounding out bigger words

LEVEL THREE Independent Reading Grades 1-3
For kids who are beginning to read on their own.

introducing paragraphs • challenging vocabulary • reading for comprehension

LEVEL FOUR Chapters Grades 2-4
For confident readers who enjoy a mixture of images and story.

reading for learning • more complex content • feeding curiosity

Ripley Readers Designed to help kids build their reading skills and confidence at any level, this program offers a variety of fun, entertaining, and unbelievable topics to interest even the most reluctant readers. With stories and information that will spark their curiosity, each book will motivate them to start and keep reading.

Vice President, Licensing & Publishing Amanda Joiner
Editorial Manager Carrie Bolin

Editor Jordie R. Orlando
Writer Korynn Wible-Freels
Designer Rose Audette
Reprographics Bob Prohaska

Published by Ripley Publishing 2020

10 9 8 7 6 5 4 3 2 1

Copyright © 2020 Ripley Publishing

ISBN: 978-1-60991-435-6

For more information regarding permission, contact:
VP Licensing & Publishing
Ripley Entertainment Inc.
7576 Kingspointe Parkway, Suite 188
Orlando, Florida 32819

Email: publishing@ripleys.com
www.ripleys.com/books
Manufactured in China in January 2020.

First Printing

Library of Congress Control Number: 2019942253

PUBLISHER'S NOTE
While every effort has been made to verify the accuracy of the entries in this book, the Publisher cannot be held responsible for any errors contained in the work. They would be glad to receive any information from readers.

PHOTO CREDITS

Ripley Readers

Sharks!

All true and unbelievable!

PUBLISHING

a Jim Pattison Company

Do you like sharks? Sharks are fish.

They live under the water.

A shark's nose is good at smelling!

That is how a shark finds
food to eat.

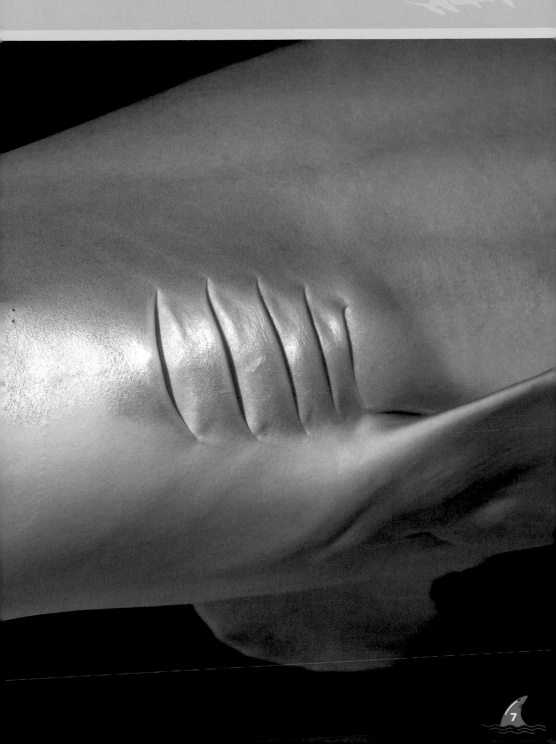

The fin on top helps a shark
swim fast.

Wow! Look at all of the big teeth!

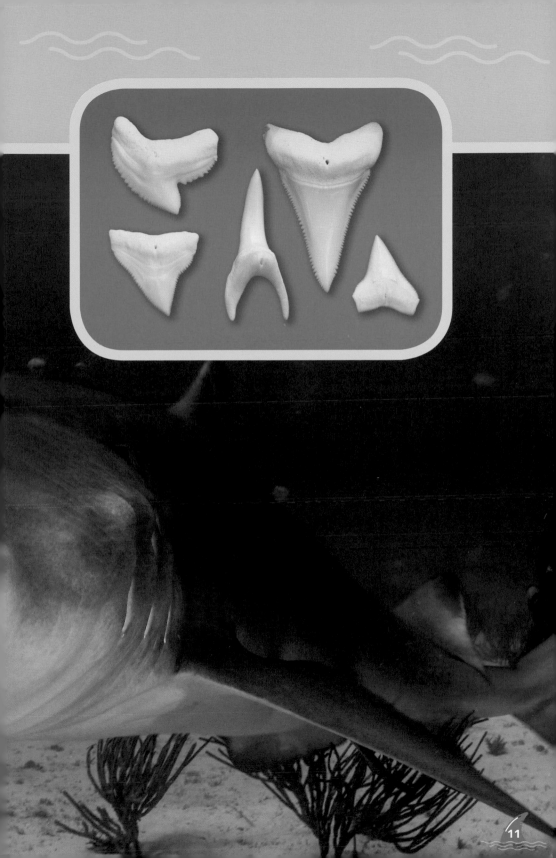

A lot of sharks like to swim alone.

Some like to swim with other sharks.

Do you see this little shark?

It is as small as your arm.

Now look at that shark!

It is as big as a bus!

Do you know what shark has a great, big body with white on its belly?

It is a great white!

The great white shark
jumps into the air
when it sees food.

Hammerhead sharks have funny faces!

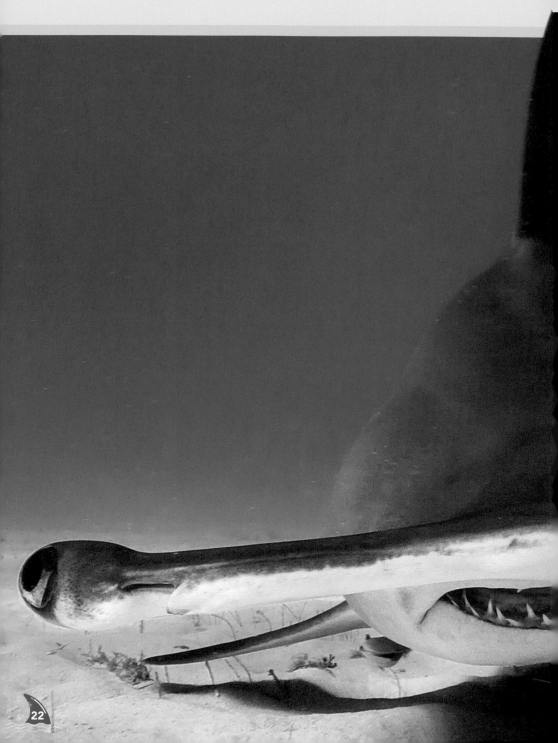

Its head looks like a hammer!

A sawfish shark has a funny nose.

Do you see how it looks like a saw?

A basking shark has a
big mouth like a net.

It eats little food that
we cannot see.

The Greenland shark can live
for 300 years.

There are so many sharks
in the world!

What shark do you like the best?

Ready for More?

Ripley Readers feature unbelievable but true facts and stories!

LEVEL ONE
Sounding it out

LEVEL TWO
Reading with help

LEVEL THREE
Independent reading

LEVEL FOUR
Chapters

Sharks!

Trucks!

Pets

Shipwrecks

Weather

Horses

Bizarre Buildings

Dinosaurs!

**For more information about
Ripley's Believe It or Not!, go to www.ripleys.com**